Images in the Clouds

reading the sky

There is Life after Academia !

Maria Wells

Marie Wells

Plain View Press, LLC
1101 W 34th Street, STE 404

www.plainviewpress.net
Austin, TX 78705

ISBN: 978-1-63210-094-8
Library of Congress Control Number: 2021922364

Cover art painting *Images in the Clouds* by Maria Wells
Interior art and photographs by Maria Wells
Cover design by Pam Knight

We Find Healing In Existing Reality
Plain View Press is a 45-year-old issue-based literary publishing house. Our books result from artistic collaboration between writers, artists, and editors. Over the years we have become a far-flung community of humane and highly creative activists whose energies bring humanitarian enlightenment and hope to individuals and communities grappling with the major issues of our time—peace, justice, the environment, education and gender.

To my daughter Sandra
for her constant and loving support, always

Acknowledgements

Three poems, "Memories in Silver," "A Poem about Poetry," and "The Child," first appeared in the Austin International Poetry Festival publication *di-verse-city 2020*.

I am grateful to my late father, Thomas A. Zevelechi, who introduced me to poetry at an early age.

To my friend Maureen Picheu, who had faith in my poetic inspiration and told me to write a poem on that night in Paris.

To my wonderful family and many friends, who supported me and believed in my poetic expression.

To Prof. John G. Herndon, for my first readings at Malvern Books, and poet Louise Richardson of Austin Poetry Society. They both welcomed me and made me feel I belonged in that wonderful world of poetry.

To David, Gloria and Elaine, who listened, encouraged and advised me with patience and humor.

To Maureen Turner Carey, for inviting me to her inspiring program of the Westbank Library Writers Workshop.

To our own Beat Poet Thom Woodruff, poets and writers Cathy S. Wilkes and Karen Johnson, Ernie Lee of New Braunfels Creative Writers, Kurt Heinzelman and Hannah Chapelle Wojciehowski of the University of Texas English Department, and Andrew Lycett, Author/Biographer from London.

To Alan Roberts, who helped me navigate the treacherous sea of computer technicalities.

And to my publisher, Pam Knight, who showed interest and enthusiasm from the start and helped me bring this project to a happy conclusion.

Contents

Remembrance

Absence

The world of poetry is slipping away
Somehow I cannot find the feeling
The inspiration
Contrasting emotions rush at me
Like beasts in a nightmare.

I am like a car that has run out of gas
in the middle of the desert
like the plane in The Little Prince
But so far no Little Prince has come to my rescue.

The source I thought would flow forever
Has dried up, no longer a soothing presence
Just a trickle, perhaps..
So I lift my hands and take those droplets
Treasure them, don't let them go

As they will be the beginning
Of a new flow
When once again, the heart will fill with memories,
Of flowers in an alpine meadow
Of children laughing
Of a man's smile
Of friends and music
Of dancing by the sea at night.
We need so little
But we do not know just
How much it was until we've lost it.

A Man Who Came to Dinner

He came promptly at 7 p.m.
Skipping the cocktail hour
He always made an entrance
And his presence
Pushed everyone else into the shadow of the room
It was as if he were the only man in the room
He radiated confidence and energy.

He enveloped you with the caress of his blue eyes
The room was empty
Except for him in the center of...longing
Candles and flowers
Silver and crystal
A table set for a Queen

But it could have been a tavern
In the middle of the desert
As long as he was there
It felt like a palace, a land of enchantment.

Sparkling wine, exquisite food
But all that mattered
Was this one presence.
He did not say much
But his voice added to the magic.

Was the food good?
I don't remember
Was the company agreable?
I could not tell, I only remember his eyes, his voice
But he left as quietly as he had come
Out into the night, taking with him a memory and a desire.
Maybe he went back to Olympus
Maybe he walked out to sea
But he never came back.

A Night in London

A foggy, drizzling night in London
Like a gray blanket softly enveloping
Buildings and bridges
The fog coming up from the Thames
Transforms the city, usually pulsing with a thousands sounds
Of people and the metallic vibrations of
Cars speeding by,
Into a dreamy stage, fit for romance and murder.

A quite night, wrapped in soft silence
The world, asleep in peaceful slumber
The streets dimly lit by the lamps
A yellow halo softening the usual brightness.

We walk, holding hands and carrying our dreams
To the end of the Earth.

A Poem About...Poetry

What is a poem?
It is an expression of hidden emotions
Hidden but not denied
It bursts out, flowing freely
Too long contained within the deep corner of a pulsing heart.
It expresses passion, pain, memories, hopes
The past and the present, a future still unknown
But full of promises.

It reveals, it heals, it tells a story, a story that is a reflection
Of this world in which we live
Or, being fearful, we choose not to live but just pass through
To live with only half our soul, half our heart, the rest dormant,
Unheard, for fear of too much emotion, too many hopes
That may be dashed, a fear of living.

But poetry, this moment of truth, frees us, and allows our soul to soar
Our heart to breathe deeply, to reach into every corners of our life
Not yet revealed, in this moment, this magic moment when
Our soul comes forth and reaches out to Heaven
To the highest, deepest, richest parts of our lives.

A Satire: a Closed Door

The old gentleman was deep in thoughts, in his small office
What to say tomorrow eager young faces looking expectantly
To absorb his every word. How thrilling!

Or was it? He was getting tired, somehow the flame was dying
His youth, inspiration, was leaving him
He went on...as usual, to meet his small world
He looked at his audience and started
Repeating words he had uttered a thousand time, how tiring
No passion in his voice.

Back in his office, he closed the door
He looked at the shelves, full of books
At the walls covered with diplomas, maybe a medal or two?
It smelled dusty, passé...soon forgotten
How could that be? Him, forgotten?
Oh yes, the world was moving on, and leaving him behind
He should build little sailboats with all his papers!
Passe'? Oh yes, it was another world.

He kept staring at that closed door
What is beyond that door?
Do I dare to open it? What unknown world is there beyond that door?
A world unknown to me
I hid in my own small, safe, world, my success closed all other doors
So what now? He was sized by a cold fear

A mocking genie swept down on him, pulled his hair
And whispered in his ear: "get up, move, open that door
There is a world out there, go, dare to be free!"
Free? Oh! But that sounds scary
What is there beyond that door?
A world unknown to me.

No, he did not dare. He wanted to sleep, to dream, just to remember
So he just sat there, and did not open that door
Until...until, there was a knock at that door

And the door opened...It was Death...beckoning to him...
Let's go...

A Silver Jewel

A woman was watering her flowers on the balcony
The child came to her and said: "Mama, look at my beautiful jewel
Silver and shiny" She lifted it to the light of the sun
It was sparkling beautifully!

The mother looked at it and shivered.
That piece of silver, she knew, she knew, how many deaths
How much destruction it had caused.

She turned to the child, worried,
"where did you find it?"
And the child replied:" Oh, no, I did not find it, Robert gave it to me,
and he has more, a box full!"

Now, the mother was angry
Robert was going to get a scolding tonight.

The lovely piece of silver
Was a splinter from a bomb
Raining down, night and day
From the silver Flying Fortresses
That came and went
Leaving death in their wake

But how could the child know?

A Stranger at the Door

Alone at home, restless
I pick up a book, I put it down
I look around, all is quiet
And reflects an order
That may hide uncertainties
A knock at the door, should not open it
The light is slowly fading
I have a fear
Of shadows in the fog outside, never friendly
But the knocking continues
I ask: "Who is there? What message
At this hour of the night?"
And the voice responds: "I am bringing you back your life."
"My life is mine, I made it!"

And the voice replies: "Yes, but you have forgotten it
I am bringing it back to you
Look at it now
I will not come back."
Maybe yes, yes, there is a lot I have forgotten
Overshadowed by bitter memories
They linger, they come to the surface
From somewhere in the past
And like waves they wash over
The walled confines of my comfort.
But now, I have to take it back
This life of mine,
Joy and sadness
Conflicts and triumphs
It has been more of a gift that a sorrow
I thank the voice in the dark
For his message
And I look at my life with a renewed awareness.

Boats Upside Down

The fishing boats were resting
In a small pebbly cove
Black tar splashed on the bottom
To preserve, protect them
During the long winters.
The cove, enclosed between a jetty and some rocks
Smelled of algae, sea water and tar
We lingered there looking out to sea
Gray and stormy waiting for the spring.

Sometimes it snowed
All the way to the edge of the sea
Black, white, the boats rested undisturbed
Except for some children
Climbing up, sliding down on to the snowy ground.

In the Spring the boats came back to life
At night you could see their lights on the horizon
And in the morning they returned to shore
With a good load and filled the market stalls with their catch
It was a ritual that repeated itself every season.

All gone now, in the winter we walk in the deserted coves
In the summer we no longer see the lights of the fishing boats on the horizon.

Where does our fish come from now?
We don't know...

Carlo Levi

He was exiled to the far end of the country
To that forgotten region, Lucania
Neither the Romans, nor the Barbarians had come this far
Neither came God nor Christ
Christ stopped at Eboli.

He did not approve of Mussolini's imperialistic aims in Africa
So he had to be silenced, cut off from any communication
With like minded men.

It turned out quite differently
Levi discovered a region ravaged by malaria
Dominated by the Church and an ancient Feudalism.

And he discovered the soul of the land
The plight of the people who he would call "my peasants"
And he painted the story of Lucania
The harsh landscape, the people, the children
He said that in Lucania he used colors he had never used before
They expressed depth, passion, a reality
These were not the portraits of the rich and famous.

With his paintings and later with his written words
He brought Lucania to the attention of Rome
And the rest of the country
And never allowed it to be forgotten.

The rebirth of the South came from his devotion
His desire to give Lucania a rightful place
Within the confines of the rest of the country.

Note: An Italian painter, Carlo Levi was exiled to a remote village in Southern Italy for his opposition to Mussolini's Imperial aims in Africa in 1935. Eight years later he would write his memories of Lucania in his book *Christ Stopped at Eboli* which compelled the Government to start a program to help the South.

Closed Houses-Empty Streets

A sense of loneliness and sadness
An absence of noises, smells voices and movement
The streets are quite, the houses closed
They do not allow a glimpse of the life within.

A garage door opens, a car drives away
The only sign that someone lives there
Behind those closed doors.

Occasionally the school bus stops
In front of a house
Children spill out giving the street
An all too brief moment of life
But then they disappear behind
Those closed doors.
And the street is silent again.

I remember my house with a terrace
And windows open to the streets
To the sun and the people
I sit on my terrace and watch the children playing
People stopping and talking.

I remember a fragrance of food
From our neighbor's kitchen
A radio playing, music there was always music.

I remember and I feel sad
As I walk along these empty silent streets.

Fear of Freedom

When the world gathered around
The altar of the leader
Deaf and blind
To the whispers of fear and caution

I did wonder
When did the ancient gates of Liberty
Shut and lock before me?

When I closed my eyes
My heart, and chose to follow a leader.

The words, liberty, daring
The words that were mine
When I had the courage to question the leadership
To look beyond the false promises
And assurances, where did they go?

The world of liberty, hope and courage
Became *"un monde dont je suis absent"*
A world in which I am absent.

But it is always easier to follow than to lead
And this was and always will be
Our sin and our failure.

Note: French from "Giorgio de Chirico" by Paul Eluard in *Mourir de ne pas Mourir*, 1924.

Golden Threads

Illusion or reality, suspended in their own world
The lovers are caught in a net
Held fast by the golden threads
Of love, intimacy and contentment.

Each thread brought them closer
As they walked together in perfect harmony.

But this closeness is sometimes challenged
By an unkind word, distance and silence

The golden threads begin to tremble, shake
And finally one by one they snap
They just lay there, on the floor, and are swept away
By a new reality.

How I Fell in Love with Poetry

Sitting on the carpet by the fireplace
In my Father's study
In our cold long winter nights
Listening to the wind
Imagining the snowflakes
Falling in the dark sky
Settling on the rooftops and chimneys.

And when Father came in
He opened the door of his library
An etched glass door with a silver key
And introduced me to poetry.

I loved the Nordic legends
With their tales of danger and mystery
Evil spirits hiding behind distorted trees
In a forest full of danger and melancholy
Engulfed in fog and silence
Interrupted only by the Wolf's cry.

So this was the beginning
Goethe's "*Erlkönig*," the King of the Elves
A Father's love, a child
And an evil King
Wanting to carry off the child to his kingdom.

"Wer reitet so spat durch Nacht und wind?
Es ist der Vater mit seinen kind"

Who is riding so late in the dark and windy night?
It is a Father with his ailing child
Riding fast in search of help
But the Erlkoning kept calling to the child
"Come with me to my kingdom
You will sing and dance with my Daughters!"

Faster and faster the Father rides
Trying to leave the forest and her evil spirits behind
But the Erlkoning comes closer, closer determined now
And he calls out "If you do not come now, I'll take you!"
The Father rides on, the forest has closed in on him now
And in his arms the child is dead.

There was a fascination in the race against Death
The presence of danger and mystery
Evil Spirits dancing
Casting their unrelenting spell
Threatening the lone traveler
It was a land of darkness and melancholy.

I was captured by it
I saw mocking spirits
Dancing in the flames of the fireplace
Reaching out caressing my imagination
I was transported into this enchanted world
And I made it mine.

Intimacy

Two people in a tender embrace
Expressing love, and everlasting hope
We believe this is intimacy
We believe that love needs a presence
That it cannot survive without a presence

But how many times in the life lived together
Two people grow distant
And retreat in a world of silence
No understanding, no exchange occurs
That would cement these two lives together
There may be a presence but the words are missing.

The intimacy that endures is a work in progress
built over a long period of time, of intimate exchanges
Of shared interests, joyful moments, concern,
Illness and doubts, reassurances and moments
Of a life intensely lived, of passion
and a growing awareness of walking on the same path.

It is intellectual, personal, it expresses love, concern
It does not expect, demand, it is like a well watered flower
A bond held together by golden threads
That can last beyond and above the demands
Of a presence, that is fulfilling, caring and giving.

Into the Canyon

We paused on the edge of the canyon
To spend the night under a canopy of stars
We could hear the coyotes calling from the other side
And in the middle a vast, dark void.

At first light it was time to descend
Into the canyon, into the thousands years
Of the world of the Anasazi

They had settled in the vast canyon of the Grand Gulch
Basket weavers and farmers
They built their houses in the alcoves
Protected from the elements
They lasted a thousand years
And they give us today an understanding
Of their lives
But why they left, remains a mystery.

For days which seem to stretch into eternity
We walked alone in this ancient world
A constant change of colors and shapes
Red and sandstone walls, boulders and small
Oasis of cottonwood trees
An occasional *tinaca* cool, blue water
A welcome break from the heat of the day.

And at night, we were overwhelmed
By a mystery unfolding
We stopped in a cave
Would the Anasazi spirits protect us or resent our intrusion?
The walls were covered with pictographs
Handprints, birds and a circle of standing figures
Holding hands, perhaps performing a sacred dance
We stood up in a circle and held hands
We felt close to the figures on the wall.

At the end, a climb on a steep wall
Regretfully leaving the canyon
At the top, we looked down
Shadows enveloping the places and the memories.

Thunder broke the silence of the night
The coyotes howled as the thunderbolts lit the sky

In a flash we saw them running along the edge
On the other side of the chasm

The canyon gave us a thunderous farewell
And then silence ......

In Trieste by the Sea

A night full of promises and consequences,
But I did not know that, then.
It all happened so spontaneously,
It simply was meant to happen.
I was not even supposed to be in that spot
That particular night.

A quiet restaurant, the sea across the street,
The red brick building of the old Fish Market
The Riviera, a long promenade by the sea
The hills ever present behind the city.

A man was sitting at a table by the door
His back to the wall, reading a book.
Trying to see the title of the book,
My interest was drawn to his face
A handsome, quiet face, a kind face.

Perhaps I was observing him too intensely,
Perhaps the book was an excuse,
He finally looked up and asked if I recognized the author
No, I did not.
So we started talking about the book and,
A bit too bold, perhaps, I asked if he would care to join us.

What a fateful decision!

It all started with a book, in a restaurant by the sea
It was a magic moment, all too brief
Full of meaning I could not foresee.

Lake Patzcuaro

On the blue surface of the lake
The fishermen were lifting
Their butterfly nets full of *pescado blanco.*

One gesture to throw the net over the water
Sideways then upward and down again
In a rhythmic movement
Repeated, all day every day
They look like they are performing a ritual dance.

Slowly, a small boat crosses the lake
And leaves us on the shores of Janitzio
A cone shaped island
It dominates the landscape
With its tall statue of Jose Maria Morelos
The Hero of the Revolution.

A steep path winds its way to the top
It is dotted with small pastel colored houses
They look like candies
Spilled out of a box, by the hand of an eager child
The gardens are full of fragrance and color.

People walk around the statue
Leaving flowers on the steps around the base
Still paying homage to the Hero of the Revolution.

At night, the Plaza in Patzcuaro is filled with music
Lights shine on the lake
Like jewels fallen from the sky.

Machu Picchu

We had reached the top of the Incas Trail, by the Temple of the Sun
In that still moment between dawn and sunrise
A soft mist shrouded the valley giving it a feeling of unreality

We looked down at the quiet and empty city
And imagined the time when it was bustling with life
People ready to start their day
With a prayer and their daily labors.

The Citadel, ordered by one, built by many
Stone upon stone in perfect harmony
Of design, beauty and endurance
These unknown builders, slaves in the Kingdom
Of an Incas ruler, worked on top of a mountain
On the upper part of the Urubamba river
A royal retreat a sacred place.

After the people left, for unknown reasons
To unknown destinations
It stood untouched, hidden from the rest of the world
And the Spanish conquerors
A vast jungle, like a green mantle
Covered the buildings, roads and fields
Machu Picchu remained buried for centuries.

And when the jungle revealed her hidden treasure
Centuries later, the men who built the citadel
Became part of her memory
And we pay homage to them today
To their artistry, their sacrifice
And we are thankful for this gift.

Memories in Silver

I look up and see this wall of silver, beautiful, sparkling, living, soft, wide, flaking, and here it comes alive and I remember as I look:

I remember my grandmother's hair, as she let it down every night, in front of the mirror and I was allowed to brush her beautiful, silver hair, lavender fragrance in the air.
Then I look again, oh, yes! These ripples in the paint, it reminds me of the waterfall by the Hotel in Badgastein: it comes down in waves and ripples and crests of silver/white and deep green on the bottom, but I looked and saw the silver in the sunlight.

And oh! The silver moon beam striking the snow, at night, lighting the path I walked in it, I danced in it and it was magic!
And there, the silver of the stars in a clear, bright night in the mountains, the gray rocks were transformed in silver cascades as they are, you know, transformed in rose petals in the sunset. Now they change, from lovely rose to lovely silver, in the light of the moon.

And this silver on the wall, the parts that come alive, as if a soft wind was moving them: how lovely, they do remind me of the decorations on my silver tea set: silver on silver, vibrant, luminous, objects of happy moments. And the little cake plates (all from Vicenza, the city of silver) and the old silver forks and knives, old but still so bright. Silver is so alive, so bright, so happy.

And there, on my dining room buffet, stand the two Sheffield silver candelabra, so ornate with little flowers and ripples just like this silver on the wall.

And then I remember a song that talks about a cat walking in the moonlight, his lovely body turned to silver: silver/white/blue...yes, there is blue in silver. And then, oh! That's a funny one: a song about a girl who liked silver so much that she climbed on the roof, with the cats, and got a lovely, silvery moon tan!

And the man with the silvery eyes with sparks of green. How I loved to look into his eyes! But, never mind, his silver eyes turned cloudy, so, I threw him away!

Oh, yes, the waves in the sea at night, I swam in the silver sea and the moon enchanted me and threw a silver beam on me. How lucky I felt so enveloped in all this silver, what a magic night!

I think of the glaciers I climbed and I remember the white being so white that it turned to silver.

And when I look back at the wall, at this silver painting, all these memories come back.

On the Way to the Water Mills

At the Pond of the Dragonflies

We drive through villages and wide valleys
The mountains ever present, majestic and reassuring.
Small churches dot their slopes and summits, white with their blue domes.
We hear the bells in the distance, calling to prayers.
And at the end of a promontory, the majestic Norman Temple of
Fotodotis, enveloped by clouds
We hear the goats bells, up the valley, but we see no goats...
Everything is a part of this mystic and solitary landscape.

And then the mountain opens up, and for a moment the sun shines on
a slope of sparkling white: the marble quarry, the precious marble used
by ancient sculptors and modern day artists.

We begin our ascent on the rocky path, one step at the time,
Keeping our balance on the uncertain terrain.
The rocks are a beautiful slate gray.
Tiny waterfalls coming down between the rocks with a soft murmur,
Above us, a canopy of soft green, darker foliage on the sides of the deep
pool, then the water falls softly into the pond below.
No sun rays filter through the leaves, but the water has its own sparkle.

The Dragonflies are restless today, they dart from one side of the
pond to the other, in search of a sunbeam.
Their colors give a flash of light: blue, red and sparkling green and gold,
their wings trembling in the air, they add beauty to this magic landscape.
Silence, only the soft flow of the water from up above the foliage, and
down to the next pool.

We are sitting on a wall surrounding the 2000 BC water mills
Butterflies softly resting on the leaves, on our hands...color and beauty
in this enchanted spot.
And then a soft sound, like raindrops falling, falling...It is my daughter,
playing the Hang Drum, and the music adds magic to the landscape.

On Mt. Olympus

The Muses were calling to me
Leave the Halls of Academia
With their empty words
Come and join us
You'll find inspiration, passion and fulfillment.

Memories, places and people were rushing at me
From past and present
Wanting to be heard
To be spoken of
To be remembered

I did remember them
And I did give them
A place in my life.

On Mt. Olympus with Calliope, Zeus, Dionysius
We toasted to Poetry
And drank Ambrosia in golden goblets
Kaki Skala, Mytikas, the summit
The music of the Heavens
Beware of Neptune, luring you
Into his kingdom of blue sea
Way down below.

The Gods and the Muses
The spirits of my ancestors welcomed me

And when it was time to descend
Guided, protected by their celestial presence
I took the enchantment with me
To my Earthly world
And I never let it go.

Pergamum

We step off the cable car
And enter the Greek city of Pergamum
The richest Kingdom of Asia Minor
A vision of white marble columns
The Acropolis, the altar of Zeus
The Temple of Dionysius
A theater sweeping down the hill
Perfect in its preserved harmony of stones upon stones.

For years, drawing these columns
With their Corinthian capitals
And ornamental acanthus leaves
Slender, fluid, curly ends gracefully folding upon themselves.
In the Art Classroom in a small town in Italy
With rows of seats coming down, as in the Greek theater
Down to the teacher's desk
We drew and dreamt of faraway places
Far in time and space
Looking at the plaster capital on the desk
And doing our best
To give a correct image to something
So beautiful and elusive.

And finally, so long after those years
I stand in front of one of my own drawings
Faithfully represented on our Fabriano paper.
I wander among columns and capitals,
One standing on the ground
Touching, caressing, sliding my hand
Down the slender fluted columns
Marveling at that perfection
Feeling, recognizing, not just seeing
Like a lover reunited with the object of his desire.

I sit on the steps of the theater
Imagining a performance, the actors
On the open stage, hearing the crowds cheer...

A hand touches my shoulder
And someone says—You are in a trance—

Yes, I am in another world
The past and the present joining together
In a moment of joyful recognition.

Riding a Bus Through the West

I found myself on a Bus, heading to Reno
Just left my friends in Austin
Standing on the Bus Station platform, waving good bye
And wishing me Bon Voyage.

The countryside, barren and lonely
Not many trees along the way
Small towns, nothing in between
It was winter, I was looking for the snow
But that would have to wait
Until we reached the North West
Days later, beyond Reno.
Stops along the way,
Sitting down at a counter of a diner
Ordering food I did not recognized
I was so far away from the familiar
So I just stuck to doughnuts.

We stopped in Las Vegas
We went into a Casino
I was advised to try my luck at the Slot machines
People laughing
Waiting for riches that would fulfill their dreams.

I put in some coins and pulled the lever and then again
Just for luck
Great excitement I had won a bunch of money
I put the money in my backpack and moved on
Back to the Bus, off to Reno
The days in Reno were filled with friends and music
Then I was on my way again through a landscape of snow and wind
All the way to Salt Lake City and Denver.

In the falling snow I thought I saw the wolves
Running along a ledge then disappearing into the night.

Solo Climb

When the mountains call you listen
And dare to ascend the highest peaks, the glaciers
It is like music inviting you to dance
Irresistible, joyful
The Via Ferrata, the Iron Way
The only way up the sheer rock wall.

Alone you begin your ascent
A long climb on the iron rungs
Fixed on the rock
You look up, one step and then another
The void on one side
Then more mountains, in an endless view
Of rocks and snowy peaks
So near you feel you can touch them
You know you are close to the top
When you feel the breeze
And snow touches your face.
.
II.
Years before this moment
A challenge I chose to take
Soldiers were fighting in these mountains
Carrying their battle gear
Up this very wall, on these steps they had secured
To be able to reach enemy lines.
More died as they fell or were buried by an avalanche
More then killed by enemy fire
More died then on the Western Front
As the ice kept secret their graves until, decades later
When the burial ground, exposed, revealed bodies
Never accounted for.
Empires fell, Nations were born
But peace did not last long.
As I climb I can hear the shots
The deadly rush of the avalanche.

I am on Sacred ground, and on the top stands a Cross
In Memoriam.

Note: I was on the climbing path, the "iron way" to reach he top of Mt. Seekofel m.2,810
in Northern Italy, the same path the soldiers built on this Eastern Front during WWI.

The Cliffs

All along the road from the Lighthouse to the Castle
The cliffs form a barrier between the sea and the houses
Attached to the side of the hill
Terrace gardens and vineyards
A profusion of colors and fragrances.

All is calm in the summer
Naked bodies dot the cliffs
Like flowers in a meadow
A joyful murmur of voices and songs.

But the winter comes with its strong wind
Sweeping down from the mountains above
Screaming down the chimneys
Hitting the windows with rain and hail.

We dare to walk along the cliffs
Challenging the force of the wind
Splashed by the waves reaching our young bodies
We lick our lips and taste the salty water

We scream with the wind, we laugh
It is a joy, fury and defiance
We are like ships in a storm at sea
We are like the seagulls flying over the waves
And we are happy, wonderfully happy.

The Child

There is a child in me
She knocks at the door of my soul
Of my heart
But I do not hear her
I am a busy woman of the world now
Memories of childhood dim and far away.
Now the world is one of
Climbing the ladder of success
Of accomplishments
Ambition
What big words we have invented to satisfy our ego
We fret and hurry
We fight and worry
And sometimes we knock someone down, climb up
And leave well behind.
But the child never gives up
She keeps calling
To pull me back from this confusing world.

And then one day my little granddaughter comes to me
She brings me a rose
She offers a candy
And we sit down on the floor
She smiles, with her soft blond curls
The sweetness and beauty of her
I look and wonder and I remember:
But this is me, just me so long ago
And she helps me retrace my steps back
To those moments of quiet beauty, pure joy.

And then I do listen to that knock at the door of my soul, my heart
And I feel restored.

The Edelweiss

In the highest mountain meadows
On sheer rocks above the graceful colors
Of the Rhododrendons and Enzians
She challenges the climber to reach her
Where eagles fly and reign supreme
And welcome only a few
Her petals are soft and velvety
Her beauty supreme.

To reach the gray peaks
Touching the bluest sky
To breath the thinnest air
To add the Edelweiss to our mountain bouquet

It is the greatest joy of a daring climber.

The Gift

What is a gift not yet received?
But consider the gifts that have filled your life:

The gift of love, of friendship and health
Of adventure, curiosity
Passion and success.

So rest your desire
And ask no more
Because there are no precious gifts
That have not yet been given to you.

As you walk along the path
Of your fulfilled life
Be generous with your gifts to others,
And give, and then your life will be richer still.

The Gypsies

On a vacant lot by my grandmother's house
The Gypsies came and set up camp
We could hear the music and the singing every night.

One night we went down to see them
They were dancing, the girls skirts swirling
Catching the wind, the boys hitting the ground
With their high boots, following the fast rhythm of the music
They were beautiful people
Such an enchanted moment.

I was five years old and I wanted to run away with the Gypsies
But the next day they were gone
I looked down from the terrace at the empty lot
And I felt very sad.

The Man Selling Christmas Trees

It was getting cold and daylight was fading
He was walking back and forth in front of the apartment building
Trying to keep warm.

A lady wrapped in furs was coming towards the building
A little boy was pulling her hand and saying:
"Mama, mama I want this tree, this big one!"
The concierge came out of the Lobby and helped bring the tree in the
building, up the elevator, into the apartment on the fifth floor
The man watched them go and was happy to imagine his tree in a beautiful
salon and children around it at Christmas Eve.

Two more trees, maybe another child would come.

But then something strange happened...
Two men were coming across the street, the two sentries who had been
walking in front of the Bunker, like him, trying to keep warm
Their guns left behind by the entrance of the Bunker,
They came to him, laughing and with signs and words indicated
That they wanted the two trees
They gave him money, more than he had asked,
They put the trees on their shoulders and carried them
across the street and into the Bunker.

Then, to his surprise, they came back to him
And with more words and gestures,
Indicated they wanted him and ...yes, "wife?" "child???"
To come tomorrow night to see his trees all lit up with bright candles
Standing in the Bunker, giving lightness and warmth
To that usually somber and cold place.

And so he did, with his wife and child, the two soldiers waiting for them
at the entrance,
The two guns, left outside, leaning against the wall
And Inside, Light and Laughter, singing and ...tears...remembering their
homes and families.
The man and his wife were offered warm wine
Cookies and a present for the child, a small bear

44

Then one soldier knelt in front of the child
showed him a picture of a child, just like him, his son
The child looked at that picture, smiled, then hugged the soldier.

A moment of peace and love, in that terrible winter of war
For the rest of his life the man never forgot this moment.

The Man with the White Crosses

He was on the road again
For sometimes now the Master Carpenter had ceased
Making tables, cabinets, toys.

Today, yesterday, and many years before
The world needed crosses, many crosses.

And he made them, big, white crosses
The names, the hearts, the flowers added later
As he placed them, where they needed to be

To mourn, to remember, to bring comfort
He had found a way to do just that
With a constant, caring, soothing gesture.

Open wide the Gates of Heaven, St. Peter,
Many are coming today

They were not ready
To leave this Earth
But someone had decided for them.

In Memory of Greg Zanis
November 27 1950 - May 4, 2020

The Snake

We were walking on a sandy path
Red canyon walls on each side
I looked down and saw the snake
Crossing the path in front of me

He was beautiful, regal
He uncoiled his body, lifted his head
He looked around shaking his rattles
They sounded like castanets.

We froze and waited
He was the King
We were the Intruders.

Squirrels and lizards
Got out of his way
He proceeded slowly
Leaving us all behind
Reaching the shelter of the rocks
Searching for water he knew was there
He belonged here

He was the King
We were the Intruders.

The Village

They came from the North to the fertile valley
To a country yet unnamed
The Romans and the Barbarians, Visigoths, Ostrogoths
Emperors and Kings, each left a mark on the land
Like footprints on the sand.

They brought language and culture
And to this day a language is still spoken
In the Northern region of the peninsula
The Ladin, a reminder of the Latin identity
Of the first Empire.

Since 1919 this part of the country has a name, Italy.
But influences remain, Germanic names,
A medieval Castle or two, hidden in a forest
Full of mystery and legends.

Orchards and vineyards
High pastures in the Alps, at the foot of the mountains
Small houses and the Church in the center of the square
Where on Sunday the Band plays
Old songs of war and mountains conquered.

Memories of childhood, of walks in the forest
Or high up in the mountain meadows
And a climb on the grey walls of the Dolomites,
Silver in the moonlight
Rose color in the sunset.

A memory of bells at noon
Sounding joyfully from the Churches in the villages
A call to the family meal
Children running down the hill
To reach home, fragrance of baked bread and fresh milk.

The farmers in the fields
Put down their scythe and shovels
And sit down for their simple meal of
Bread and bacon, then a drink at the cool spring
Warm summers, full of games and songs
And poetry, there was always a moment
For poetry.

The Waterfall

We walked softly into the woods
On a path of flowers and fallen leaves
A canopy of green above our heads
The sun rays breaking through the leaves
And leaving a touch of gold
As the breeze moved the branches
From shadow to sunlight.
At the end of the path a pond of deep green-blue water
Sparkling against the high rock wall.
The waterfall, white and silver rushing down from the edge
The beauty and calm of the place
A moment of rest, the soothing coolness of the water.

As we turned slowly,
Looking up at the crest of the cliff
At the rushing water,
We saw a bush, a tree a rock falling, followed by another
And yet another, bigger boulders
Falling down, following the path of the waterfall
Taking along trees, rocks, a snake a squirrel
Twisting and turning along the edge of the water.

A last image against the blue sky
And it all crushed into the pond
Turning the water into a muddy brown
Overflowing onto the shores
A vision of fear
A need to flee this place
So changed by the sudden fury of Nature.

There Was a City

Bombs falling
Houses crumbling
Like a deck of cards
Pushed by an angry hand
Ruins in the streets
A wall with a window
Still held on its frame
Like an eye looking into the void.
A curtain hanging
Torn and limp, a pattern of bright flowers
Still claiming
A last breath of life.
Unmoved the sun still shone
Through the dust, with an attempt
Of comfort and warmth.

A doll, sitting among the ruins
Where was the child who had rocked her?
A piano still standing
Against a wall with ripped wall paper
But no one to play
Too difficult to reach up there
High above the street
But no stairs.

Children playing among the ruins
Picking up bomb splinters
No one calling to them
No one aware of the danger
Dazed by the spectacle of the wounded city.

A woman, holding a child by his hand
Was murmuring to him "we go home now
Up on the hill
Away from this desolation."

Those Lonely Sunday Afternoons

I remember sitting by the window
At my grandmother's house
Looking across the street
At the children playing in the soccer field by the school.

A fragrance of baking bread coming from the kitchen
Preparing for an evening meal
Who will be there tonight?
We seem to have lost the habit
Of a family gathering
Everything is different since my grandfather died.

Why was I there, alone? I don't remember
My parents must have gone out, somewhere
But would they come back tonight?
Will everyone come back tonight
To my grandmother's kitchen?

Voices from the street, children laughing
A song from a radio next door
But above all a deep, inexplicable melancholy.

Why was I there alone?

Trieste Memories of a City

Trieste, a beautiful city nestled between the mountains
and the sea
Row boats and sail boats crossing the silvery/blue Adriatic
in the morning,
And at night, a thousand lights, trembling on the far horizon
of a dark sea, the fishing boats... bringing in a good catch
in the morning.
The house wives rushing to the fish market to get the best
of the display of shimmering, trembling, colorful offerings
swordfish and crabs, lobsters and shrimps, all moving and alive
The market stalls in the square,
colorful, fragrant, the vendors offering their fare
the house wives picking the best, plump fruits
the freshest greens. A lively place to shop, linger and gossip
In the Fall, the fragrance of the roasted chestnuts, warm and delicious,
we hold the sac, warming our hands.

And Maximilian, Joyce, Svevo, Saba... their ghosts wander
the streets, meet in the old café, read their last poem
a chapter of their book....
Joyce prefers the Old City, the taverns in the port, drinking with the
sailors, exchanging jokes, telling Irish legends, singing along with the
sailors, yes, Joyce did sing...
Joyce's children, Giorgio and Lucia, rush to meet him, when he comes
home, but he sends them off and sits at his desk and writes, writes...his
first chapters of Ulysses...
A white marble sign on his house, a testament to his creation in a small
corner of an enchanted city.

Maximilian wanders in the gardens of his beloved Miramar
The castle he built for his dear, adored Carlotta
On a promontory overlooking the sea
it looks like it is ready to go into the unknown, like his equally beloved
ships.

But it was to be a short honeymoon...the call to power, the Imperial Crown of Mexico. "Do not listen, Maximilian, said the poet, don't listen to the Chimera of this distant land, stay with us, Maximilian!"
But Carlotta was restless in the gardens of Miramar
she wanted to be Empress of Mexico.... and so they left...
on their ship, Novara, the same ship, that just a few years later would bring his coffin back to Trieste.
He was shot on the hill of Queretaro, and his memory lives on in Trieste.

A city of dreams and recollections
Of a romantic and troubled past
In the narrow streets of the Old City
Leading to the hill of San Giusto, the Patron Saint
Small houses in ancient stones still survive

Memories always present, the city comes to life
And speaks to you, and never lets you forget.

This is the beauty of this city, but also her powerful spell...she just does not let you go, not completely, not ever.

Note: Joyce lived in Trieste from 1904 to 1915.

When the Guns Fell Silent

France 1914

Snow had been falling for days
On the trenches, on the battle fields
In that cold night of December 24th
The men were waiting for the next assault
But a song rose in the night
From the German lines a man emerged
Singing "Silent Night" carrying a small tree
Lit with candles, a reminder of home, of the Holy Night
He crossed the line and came towards the French and British trenches
Followed by his men
Joining him in the song.

Slowly, unsure at this unexpected sight
The British, French, Scots came up and joined the Germans
A Scottish soldier accompanying the singing with his bag-pipe.

And soon they were all surging from their trenches,
Like the ghosts on Bald Mountain leaving their graves
Joining in a merry Sabbath.

In a moment, they were all greeting, embracing
Sharing gifts from home
They were men again not soldiers
The war was young, just five months
It had killed men, but it had not yet killed the spirit.
And on that night when the Child Christ was born
There was no battle, in that moment
Humanity prevailed and they were in peace.

As the spirits on Bald Mountain returned to their graves
When the Church bells announced the new day
The soldiers gave themselves another day
To bury their dead, to linger for a moment longer
To wish one another a Christmas Day without
The specter of death.

And then the battles resumed on the Western Front
And that brief peace was shattered.

A Touch of Humor

A Child Is Born

Too soon, unexpected today
She interrupts vacation plans
Grand Opera at the Arena in Verona
Baby clothes had not yet been delivered
From some fancy stores.

Champagne cases still unopened
Were just sitting on the floor
In the dining room
A name had not been chosen
Aunts and uncles battled
To have their choice approved
Brother Robert wants to call her Marie Rose.

Father rushed back from the mountains
His second climb of the summer interrupted.

The baby girl laid peacefully in her mother's arms
Totally unaware of the commotion she had caused.

And when the father arrived, he held her in his arms
Lifted a glass of Champagne, finally delivered
He dipped his finger in the glass
And put it on the child's lips
She sucked it happily and acquired a taste for it.

The Gods came down to Earth from Olympus
In their golden chariot to give this child
Their blessings and their gifts
They gave her a name Thalia
The name of one of the three Graces.

It's a Girl!

For my granddaughter Lucia

I am but two days old,
My name is Joy
At least I think so
I hear this voice repeating,
She is such a Joy!
There is laughter and voices
And, again: She is such a Joy!

And they bounce me and kiss me,
And tickle me
And bathe me and dress me...
Dress me ? Why do I need that??

I blink and grimace,
Trying to convey my discontent
But a voice is saying
Oh, look she is laughing
She is looking at me!
No I am really not looking at anyone,
Oh dear, it was so nice and quiet
Where I came from!

Time passes, I am taken into a big bright place,
And I am dressed from head to toe
Dress, booties and a bonnet
I try to loosen the ribbons,
I am so uncomfortable.

Finally they do take off my bonnet
And they bend me over a big tub
Surely they cannot give me a bath now,
I am all dressed up!

But then, someone pours cold water over my head!
I scream! Wouldn't you??

Mercifully, they dry me, but then the
bonnet is back.
A tall figure in a white robe
Places his finger on my forehead and says:
Lucia, Sabina, Grace
Oh I like that, yes, I like Lucia.

But there comes that voice again
Oh, she is such a Joy!

Wait a minute, didn't you hear the tall figure in the white robe
Call me Lucia?
Stop calling me Joy!

Noise and laughter, and light
All so very tiring...
I do need to sleep.

I am two weeks old,
And my name is Lucia.

At the Gates of Heaven

I presented myself to St. Peter
Asking to be admitted
He motioned to his angel assistant
To give me the few items I was entitled to
A white flowing robe, a halo, wings and a harp
I tried to refuse the harp
As I assured them I could not play
But Peter said, no matter, you will play
If you say so Peter, you may regret it
But please assign me on a cloud a bit away
From other harp playing souls, as I am very sensitive to sound.

I remember what Capitan Stormfield told me about the racket
Of all these souls playing the harp
When they were clearly not inclined to musical expression.
As I was settling on my cloud, adjusting my crown, wings and robe
I heard a voice coming up all the way from Earth
It seemed I had left some unresolved issues
So my presence was required back on Earth.

I run to Peter and asked to be given a three days pass
He frowned and fussed a bit
But in the end he gave me this pass
And I sped back to Earth
Most unwillingly to solve some human problems
Which, seen from Heaven, seemed totally irrelevant.

But kindness prevailed and I returned for a moment
To old feelings, uncertainties, misgivings...
Nothing was settled nor improved, of course
But I was sure that my extraordinary effort
Would at least show that even in Heaven
I cared for the dear ones I had left behind
In their perpetual confused status.

Note: *Capitan Stormfield 's Visit to Heaven* by Mark Twain, 1909.

The Devil's Tail

In recent times, the World seems to be
The target of an angry God
Jupiter himself, tired of the foolishness of men
Was striking the Earth with his thunderbolts
From Olympus.

But no, he was wrongly accused
Actually the other Deity, the Fallen Deity, Lucifer
Was expressing his discontent
With the humans of this world.

He liked them mean, devious, treacherous
But not stupid, definitely no.
He had no patience with stupidity
He was quite disappointed with them
As, instead of fighting the enemies
Which would have left a battlefield full of bodies
And souls for his picking,
Men were fighting among themselves
With Words, alas!
So the devil decided on a course of action
Not known but quiet effective.

He had accumulated all the ills of the world,
Gathered in millennia of wondering the many parts of the Earth.
And stored them neatly on his tail.

So now, energized by his anger
He went flying high into the world
Shaking his tail violently, left and right
Up and down, and as he shook and sped, all the ills went flying down to
Earth causing havoc and despair.

And the Devil, freed of the burden of the ills of the world
and a heavy burden it was
Run back to the comfort and warmth of Hell, ready to relax.

My! It was cold in the world!

Fantasia

A Glass of Water

I am standing by a white plate, at the Taverna,
I am pretty, clear glass, like the ice cubes in my water, but I am special
I have a blue rim and no one else does, that distinguishes me....

A man comes and picks me up, no grace in his movement,
And he throws my water on someone's head!
How shocking! I was not meant for such violent acts...I do not approve,
no, not at all..
Someone restores my water... I feel better..

A child comes and sits at the table
With her little lovely hands, she lifts me and holds me..
It feels like a caress...she holds me gently, to take a sip, with her rosy cool
lips...it feels like a kiss, I bend over a bit to help her drink,
She is so careful, with a serious expression on her small beautiful face.

Then she puts me down, takes a pitcher, and pours more water, very
thoughtful indeed.

A lady comes and drops a white tablet in my water, it is bubbling, tingling,
sparkling....it spills over my rim, it makes me sneeze...but what a cool,
nice feeling!

It is wonderful to be of so many uses, I feel needed, and I like to sit at the
bedside table, at night, and offer my water to a feverish child.

I am so important, why, yes, man can do without many things but he
cannot live without water...I am the source of life for Man and Earth.
I feel like dancing, my water swirls around with ice cubes clicking
A cool, joyful sound.

A Golden Cage

A Golden Cage
was sitting in the Great Hall of the Royal Palace
A beautiful bird posed gracefully on his perch

Black, lustrous feathers
A spot of white on his head
Like a crown of distinction
Maybe he was a King
In the distant land where he came from.

He was singing wistfully, a melancholy song
An echo of the jungle in a distant land
It conveyed sadness and longing.

Maybe one day someone will open the door
Of the Golden Cage and the bird will fly back
To his enchanted land.

But there is another kind of Golden Cage
Where people choose to dwell
A Golden Cage of Privilege and Power
Those living inside this Golden Cage
Know nothing of the pain and labors
of the people living beyond its confines
And they like it so.

They live with their eyes turned away from
What is called Reality
An unpleasant, unsettling word they prefer to ignore
Their isolation, their distance from any touch of reality
Is their armor.

Closed in, living their life as on a single note
They are unmoved and unaware
Their safety in this ignorance of things
Beyond their care.

But beware because the crowds are gathering
By the gates and will, one day crash through
The door of the Golden Cage
And end this life never truly lived.

Dancing on the Beach

The musicians had left the Taverna
They came to the beach
Their Bousouki vibrating with music
The Sirtaki, the Rembe'tiko
Every song, every memory was played for us.

And we danced
In that magic moment
When the sea turns from red to silver
In the light of the moon
We danced
And the dolphins danced

Their bodies turned to silver
And the stars danced in the dark blue sky
The children danced on the rocks above the beach
The Priest came dancing out of his church
The bells laughed merrily
Joining the joyful celebration
In the light of the moon.

And we danced
At the edge of happiness
We joined the dolphins
Following them in the moon beam.

And the Gods smiled down at us
From Olympus.

Diamonds in the Grass

On a quiet summer evening
I saw diamonds in the grass
Bright lights twinkling among the grass blades
They were sparkling in silver and gold
They seemed to be moving, gathering into a cluster of great brilliance.

But then, I looked closer—they were no diamonds
They were fireflies
Then I remembered a children song about fireflies

"Come and light my path lovely fireflies
And I will protect you
From the hidden dangers of the night."

Foglie Morte

Against a soft grey sky
A burst of color, the leaves of autumn
Red, yellow and brown
Dancing in the wind
They softly settle on the ground
On our hands
On our faces turned up to the sky.

Some will grace the marble floors
Of a great Hall
Falling from crystal vases.

We call them "Foglie morte" dead leaves
Oh, but we forget
How much life they will bring forth in the Spring.

They will nourish the ground below the trees
The Earth will lay silent and dark
In the cold winter.

But a bright new life
Will spring forth
And we will marvel
At the new splendor.

High Tide-Low Tide

Standing at the edge of the water
Warm sand caressing my feet
Wavelets playing between my toes.

High Tide, a warm embrace
Soothing movement of the sea
All is calm and in harmony with the Universe.

But the moment passes
Low Tide, the sea retreats
Sucking away the sand from under my feet.

I stand alone, unbalanced
At the edge of the Blue

A sense of abandonment
Sweeps over me.

Images in the Clouds

Reading the Sky

I was lying down by the pool
the breeze playing in the rose bushes
petals moving softly, settling on the grass.

But when I looked up, at the sky
at the clouds, a whole world of moving images appeared
softly moved by the gentle breeze.
The lacy, white puffs of clouds, forming a firmament of their own
begun to fill the sky with an endless variety of moving images
and, as the breeze was gentle, the images formed and vanished
only to create a new image, slowly and softly
you could hold the image in your eyes long enough to enjoy it
each one with a certain personality
for as long as the breeze allowed it to stand still
and then, it softly rolled away, to form still another image.

Here comes a fierce dog, his ears pointed, his paws stretched forward
as if to clutch a small, white puff that kept moving away from him
his eyes, set deep in his face, his hair standing up on his head.
But then comes the breeze, and the dog vanishes
only to become, wonder of the sky
a woman, with a head full of hair, all puffed up on top
and a veil trailing behind her
one arm moving forward, to catch another cloud
as if she wanted to add a touch of elegance to her figure
and small puffs formed in the wake of her veil, as babies
following her in line
Some had little round heads, some little legs and feet
and they seemed to be dancing on her veil.

But a stronger breeze comes and makes these separate images
blend in one big....monster!
spiky hairs, a big face, a cruel smile
the sides of his mouth turned up
and as the breeze kept touching it, changing its contours
the smile turned into a grimace
but then, the breeze turned to wind, and the monster toppled backwards,
his legs stretched to the sky
until it was swallowed by a big uniform cloud
that swept all images away

then the sky was blue, silent, empty
the images had all flown to the mountain
maybe to join Zeus and Dyonisus, for their pleasure
Mt. Zaas disappeared in the clouds
And the sky was still.

Men are as Waves in the Sea

They erupt in a joyful dance one moment
Then they are crushed onto some rocks
Pushed by the force of an unexpected storm
Perhaps they find a rock to land on
Perhaps they are pushed back to sea.

In the sea of Life
Nothing is permanent, safe, secure.

If men have attained pleasure
Sadness is not far away
Because sadness is a sister to pleasure.
Men are always challenged
Perhaps this is what makes them strong
But they must always look out
For that rock to land on.

Theseus, Ariadne and Dionysious

A Betrayal and a Rescue

Theseus was victorious, he had killed the Minotaur
In the Labyrinth on Crete, and made his way out
with the help of Ariadne's thread.

He said to Ariadne, "Come with me, we'll sail back
To my Kingdom and you will be my bride."
And Ariadne replied, "Yes, my King"
And off she went with Theseus, sailing away
on his beautiful ship.

After many days at sea,
They stopped at the island of Naxos
On the promontory, by the mighty Arch of Augustus.
There, lulled by the sun, and the sound of the waves
Ariadne fell asleep.

And Theseus sailed off without her!
When Ariadne woke up and found herself all alone,
she cried and cried....oh! What to do?

But Dionysius, the God of wine, lust and merrymaking
Spotted her from his seat on Olympus
Oh, what a lovely maiden!
So down he swooped and came to her and said:
"Why are you all alone and sad?
Come with me to Olympus and be my bride, we will make merry, drink,
dance and sing!"
It all sounded quite lovely, and she went to Olympus with Dionysius.

Theseus was sailing back to Athens
And when, to announce his safe return
He was to hoist the white sails, the black sails went up instead

Theseus's father at the sight of the black sails, sign of mourning, believing
his son dead, in desperation
Threw himself from the Acropolis and plunged into the sea.

And Theseus became King.
It must have been the will of the Gods!

The Ball

The young Duke of Richmond was sitting in the salon
Of his family Palace enjoying his evening cocktail.

He was looking at his family portraits
And musing over the stories
Of their brilliant and turbulent lives
The balls, the intrigues the heroes and the villains
The lives lost at Waterloo
Perhaps he should give a ball this winter
But in his modern world
Balls had gone out of fashion
His friends were now into jazz club and macarena
Too bad, no balls for us.

The lovely ladies in the portraits leaned forward
To look into the portraits next to them
One asked—did the Duke mentioned a ball?—
Yes, he did
We should have a ball again
Like on that night, on the eve of Waterloo
Let's open the doors of the ballroom.

Suddenly, charmed by this idea
They all begun to step off their frames
They gathered in the salon
Joyfully greeting one another
Then they moved forward
And opened the mirrored doors of the ballroom.

The chandeliers were blazing with a thousand candles
The music invited all to join in a quadrille, a waltz a mazurka
The ladies, escorted by their handsome Officers of the Red Guard
Moved gracefully, lightly posing their gloved hands
on their partner's shoulders.
Promises were made, love vows exchanged
But when the call to battle was heard
They begun to disperse, lost and fearful
The music lingered to accompany their sorrowful retreat
Then the ball room was empty again, the doors closed.

The Duke awoke, he had a dream
He thought he heard music coming from the ballroom,
He opened the doors and went in
There was a fragrance in the air of candle wax and jasmine, roses and gardenias

He looked down, and saw a gardenia on the floor.

The Painter's Room

Spider webs hanging from the crooked beams of dark wood
against the ceiling,
They form a light gray pattern that add a touch of décor,
in the corner of the room, giving it a feeling of warmth,
not of solitude or chill.

On a wood paneled wall, a window, broken glass, it looks like it was put
there by mistake, and then forgotten by the sun rays
and the blue of the sky.
In this moment, only a light wind comes through the window
a cold whisper that chills the weak flames of the stove
standing alone in the middle of the room.

A man was busy, in a corner of the room, with some old empty bottles:
He was looking for something to paint: he liked to paint what was reflected
on the smooth, green glass of the bottles.

All around him, canvasses, a picture completed or just begun: the images
reflected on the bottles, the small window, a mouse, all the things that
were around him in the small room.
He was alone and could not walk
He could never paint the beautiful and colorful world
outside his prison of dark beams and light spider webs.

So he painted the reflection of that world, as it came into the room and
settled on the smooth glass of the bottles.

Note: I wrote a short story in Italian, translated it into English, then wrote this poem.

The Sound of Silence

The flaming sunset has subsided
The sun has gone down
Behind the mountain
On the island across the sea.

The waves splash against the rocks
With a soft murmur

All is quiet, as the world stands still.

Earth and Sea awaken
And on this night
Ask you to pause, and listen to the sound of Silence.

The birds chirp in the cedar trees
Beyond the rocks

A branch breaks and falls
A cat meows in distress
And reaches for another branch

Two owls call to each other
A frog croacks in the fountain by the Church
A waterfall sings, and splashes between the rocks
And fills the pond below.

Listen, listen to the whisper of Earth and Sea
What does it matter if we have suffered
Nature follows her course
Her notes now black, now white

Somewhere we find a moment of peace
If we listen to the Sound of Silence.

The Stone Garden

A quiet neighborhood
A cool morning walk up and down the hills
Meeting friendly dogs and curious squirrels
Running down a tree to see what's new on the street
Waiting for a nut, looking at me expectantly.

The dog, always on the same front steps
Comes to meet me in hope of a conversation
Very friendly, he walks with me
I talk to him, he listens with kind understanding
It is good to confide in small animals
They always listen, patiently
And the trees look down with approval.

It is so peaceful in the morning with the animals and trees
An occasional cat, but he is rather suspicious and does not stay long
I find myself talking about may day
My fears, my sorrows and my joys
It is so easy to confide in them and myself
In this moment of undisturbed solitude.

Something beautiful reveals itself
At the foot of a tree
In a small garden patch set back from the road
A Stone garden, with messages inscribed
Paintings, lovely words of friendship love, hope.

The neighbors have found an unusual way
To communicate with one another
To express their thoughts, to say—we are all here—

I pause, I read and I place my stone among the others
It has a painting of a village
And a simple message "With love".

The Train of Life

I got on the train at midnight
I headed for the bar
People sitting around, talking,
each one with a story to tell.

I was not sure I got on the right train
I did not know where this train was heading

But it was going fast, too fast
I did not know if I had a choice
whether I was a conductor
or a simple passenger.

I could not stop it, I could not get off
As that would have meant the end of it all,
The end of my voyage.

I did not want that
I still wanted to give a chance
To the train of my Life.

Note: Inspired by a line in a French book *Spirales* by Tatiana de Rosney in which the character is caught in the consequences of her actions and feel as if she were "*sur un train …lance' a toute vitesse…*" And getting off would mean giving up life.

To Market

I went to market today
There was not much there to choose from.

I found sadness, melancholy, frustration, loneliness
I made a bouquet and brought it home.

It gave out an unpleasant fragrance
Heavy, somber.

After a while I went to market again
And this time I found compassion, forgiveness
Contentment, gratitude.

I made a bouquet and brought it home
Its fragrance was sweet, strong
And it restored the lightness in the room.

The first bouquet begun to wither and die,
One petal after the other
And that was the last we saw of it.

Tonio Kroger a Memory of Youth

In the noisy cheerful crowd of children laughing and dancing
I isolated myself as I often did and I went to the window
There I quietly looked out into a world of melancholy grey
Of wind and waves
The landscape of the Northern sea.

A boy was walking on the beach alone
It was cold, why was he there?
Why did he choose loneliness
Why did he part from his companions?
He felt serene suspended between the sea and the shore
He felt understood in this solitude.

The wind enveloped him with a cool caress
He heard the spirits of the Northern legends
Whisper in his ears, he walked closer and closer to the sea

A wave reached out and touched him
A sense of danger of the overpowering forces of Nature
Overwhelmed him, and he stopped...but what happened?

Tonio Kroger turned back to the room
The window was closed
He had been looking into his soul
Into the depth of his lonely soul.

Note: Inspired by Thomas Mann's *Tonio Kroger*, 1903.

The Wall

I was going somewhere
I don't remember where
Along the way I stopped
And leaned against a wall.

The cool stones felt good
Against my weary body
In the silence I could hear
The Church bells from the village
In the valley below.

And then I heard whispers, voices near me
They asked to be heard
I stood still and listened
Each one had a story to tell.

The wall was a resting place for some
Then they moved on into the unknown
In hope of finding fulfillment, success
That they had not been able to find
Where they came from.

The wall was a transit point in their lives
But what was there, beyond the wall
That would make their long journey worth taking
Was there really something far better
On the other side of that wall?

In that moment of stillness
They saw a life lived
With only half their soul
Half their heart
Then they realized that the power
Of enriching their lives
Was within themselves,
Not in another place
Not in an imagined world
Not far away beyond this wall.

The Whirling Dervishes

It was not a stage
It was not a public performance
We had entered a temple
The world of the Sufi sacred dance
Mysterious music, graceful movements.

To watch in silence and experience
The beauty of this dance
We were entranced
Elevated into a higher sphere
Something beyond our worldly experience
Like the spirit of a sacred lantern
Lifting itself into space
I felt my soul leaving my body
Following the dance.

And I whirled with the Dervishes
The music, so soft and yet so compelling
I could not stop, I felt transported
Soothed, blessed
And when, at the end my soul returned to me
When the music stopped, and the white figures
Their light gowns no longer in motion
A silence returned to the place, an immense peace
And I carried it away with me
Restored and whole as if I had for a moment
Inhabited the sacred space of the Sufi.

And when we left, we silently returned to our world
Treading lightly, more conscious of the sublime.

Note: A memory of a night in Cappadocia.

Comments from Poets and Writers

I like "Memories in Silver" a lot. I like what you are asking your readers to do, which is to picture things that may or may not be silver *becoming* silver in a certain light. The cat in the moonlight is particularly striking. The grandmother's hair, silver and scented with lavender, sets the mood of the poem early on. We are travelling backward in time to many places, exploring events that remain vivid and striking in memory. The poem invites the reader to recall past events and give them a silver overlay, so that they too become precious. It invites us to treasure our own life experiences, which we can transform through a memory exercise that reevaluates and accepts the past.

Like the previous, "The Child" shares a journey backward in time with the reader. It's very direct in the way that it asks the reader to imagine the narrator with her grandchild, who calls her back to her much younger self. We do the same. It's a wonderful feeling that I get from this poem. There is a feeling of generativity, hopefulness, and continuity of family, but also of self.

"High Tide-Low Tide" and "The Train of Life"—I love these poems. They leave me with strong feelings. Each of the poems conveys an embodied experience that I can feel vicariously. I really like that, and I like the emotions that go with those experiences."

—Hannah Chapelle Wojciehowski, Professor of English, The University of Texas at Austin

"It's a Girl!" is an original, unexpected stream of consciousness or "*monologue interieur.*" Evoking a newborn's emerging identity! "When the Guns Fell Silent" is nicely evocative and soothing, underscoring a peaceable moment in a war context.

—Jean -Pierre Cauvin, Professor Emeritus of French Literature

I absolutely love "The Cliffs". What a glorious picture you have painted, with all the emotions between tranquility and chaos, and captured within a few short lines. I do subscribe to the "less is more" school of thoughts.

—John M. Knapp, London/Muscat

"Stone Garden" is just beautiful! I enjoy my morning walks, alone, sometimes thinking, sometimes praying. You have expressed what I see so beautifully. Thank you for reminding me to notice all these glorious little snippets of life.

—Karen Johnson, Poet, New Braunfels Creative Writers

"The Whirling Dervishes"—I was enthralled by the idea of your spirit leaving your body as you witness this. I also loved when the dancing ended and your spirit returned, how you were changed, "more conscious of the sublime" It seems that something beautiful transports you and the experience of witnessing it elevates you.
—**Maureen Turner Carey,** Writers Workshop Organizer, Westbank Library

Maria Wells is an accomplished observer of the human condition in many countries. She has travelled much, and observed more than most. Her poems are luxury travel. Her first hand experiences thrill, amaze and delight. Let her poems guide you through Greek Mythology, and take you to Olympus!
—**Thom Woodruff**, SPIRIT THOM, Beat Poet Laureate of Texas 2020-2022

"Solo Climb" is very rich in imagery and metaphor, and it evokes the Gods. I felt I was climbing and striving with you, not worrying about reaching the peak but ever making my way upward because there was no other way to go but upward.
—**Louise Richardson**, Poet, Austin Poetry Society

"How I Fell in Love with Poetry" and "Tonio Kroger, a Memory of Youth" both capture the bleak beauty of the Northern landscape and seas, and how it is part of the Nordic heritage. They also remind me of the Blues—the seeming paradox of being warmed and enamored by facing the cold, danger and death; of feeling understood in facing solitude. And your art in being able to give voice to those seeming paradoxes and to bring me into your public performance of them, this again is the art of the Blues.
—**Peter Philippson**, M.Sc. Psychotherapy trainer, writer, UK

About the Author

On Mt. Zaas, Naxos Island

A Fulbright Scholar and Doctoral graduate from the University of Pisa, Maria Xenia Wells Zevelechi spent her career at the University of Texas at Austin. Her academic books include: *The Ranuzzi Manuscripts, Italian Post-1600 Manuscripts and Family Archives in North American Libraries, The Italian Collections across the Centuries: Literature, Art* and *Theater, and Aldine Press Books at the Harry Ransom Humanities Research Center.* She has published articles about ancient manuscripts, modern Italian authors, dialect poetry, art and Puppet Theater. The World Catalog Identities confirms 15 works in 36 publications in two languages held in 363 libraries worldwide. The Italian Government awarded her the title of Cavalier in the Order of Merit of the Italian Republic. She has traveled extensively to conferences in the US and Europe and explored the countries of Morocco, Turkey, Peru, Russia.

After retiring from Academia, Maria embraced poetry. Her first poem, "Memories in Silver" was inspired by a friend's painting and written while in Paris at a meeting of Poets and Writers. A member of Austin Poetry Society, Maria first published some of her poems in the Austin International Poetry Festival publication *di-verse-city 2020.* She gives readings in Austin, Paris and Greece.

With two daughters, five grandchildren and the memory of a loving husband who encouraged her to see anything as possible, she lives in Austin, Texas and often visits family in Italy and Greece.

CPSIA information can be obtained
at www.ICGtesting.com
Printed in the USA
LVHW070052290122
709614LV00001B/1